2.98

London before the Blitz 1906-40

Graham Norton

Contents

Jacket illustrations

front: a Buckingham Palace garden party in 1919
back: Edwardian street urchins
inside flap: Holborn in 1912

© London Weekend Television. Macdonald & Co. (Publishers) Ltd., 1970. SBN 356 03433 X

First published in 1970 by Macdonald & Co. (Publishers) Ltd.,
St. Giles House, 49 Poland Street, London, W.1

Made and printed in Great Britain by Hazell Watson & Viney Ltd., Aylesbury, Bucks

London before the Blitz 1906-40

from the coming of the motor-car to the outbreak of war

by Graham Norton

Macdonald, London

A dramatic glass curtain building, built for the Express newspapers in 1931. Its black glass panels set in chromium strips create an exotic and sophisticated image, a perfect advertisement for the newspaper that Beaverbrook built up between the wars.

Introduction

The twentieth century saw London lose its self-confidence. Like the British Empire itself, Londoners had been so sure of themselves. Around them were their monuments, terraces and squares, the Houses of Parliament, Tower Bridge, the Bank of England, symbols of a world-wide system, in which London was the directing brain, the beating heart. Unquestionably, this was the biggest and richest city in the world.

London was inviolate. No foreign enemy had entered her gates since William of Normandy. During the Napoleonic Wars, nearly every other major European city had seen the triumphant entry of a conqueror. Within the memory of most Londoners living in the first decade of our century, Paris had been bombarded and looted in 1870. It could never happen here, was the general feeling. Now the realisation was dawning that the time might not be too far distant when Britain and its capital would be in peril from a new threat by sea and even, for the first time in history, in the air.

The challenge came. In August 1915, the Germans bombed Leyton. In September, the airships were over the City itself and its streets blazed. All through the war, casualties from the massacres in the Flanders trenches poured into Victoria and Waterloo. By 1918, there was hardly a family in London which had not lost a father, a son or a brother at the Front. No longer, as in the first phase of the war, did the seaports, the county regiments and the Highlanders bear the major part of the life-sacrifice. Now everyone was involved.

Things could never be the same after victory had come. The bulk of the world's gold, which had for the most part been permanently lodged in the vaults of the Bank of England, found a new home in America's Fort Knox. Poverty and industrial unrest made a sombre counterpoint to the wild parties of the West End's 'Bright Young Things' in the 1920s. The thirties, though they saw a distinct improvement in the health and living conditions of Londoners, were years clouded by waves of unemployment and the increasing threat of a war which now might altogether wipe out London. Little wonder that those who in 1940 could remember that first Edwardian decade, when total war was unimaginable, looked back to it as a golden age.

A Salvation Army worker feeds destitute children. The 'Sally' Army, founded originally by William Booth in 1878 with the sole aim of saving souls, became increasingly concerned with welfare work—with the crusade against the ills bred by urban poverty. Most slum children grew up undernourished, dirty and unhealthy.

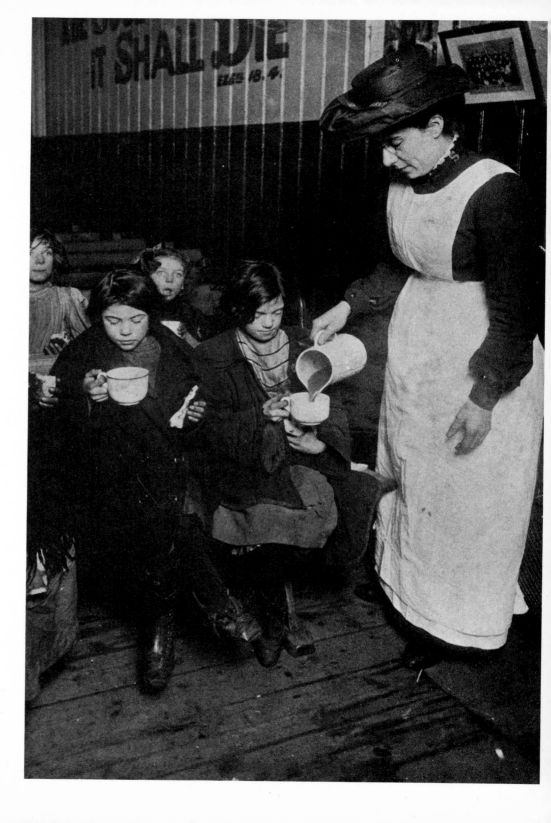

Edwardian London

Queen Victoria died on January 22, 1901, and was succeeded by her eldest son, Edward VII, by now in his sixties, but with an unquenched zest for life and a pretty woman. At first there was little to mark either the new reign or the new century. The king might be a more raffish character than his exemplary mother, but the change in the moral climate at Buckingham Palace only reflected the generally more permissive social attitudes which had come in with the 1890s. Then, as Prince of Wales, Edward had been the acknowledged leader of the smart set, and most of his friends were now as welcome at the Palace as they had been at Marlborough House.

But by 1906, change was in the air. That year was the true watershed of time which divides our own century from the one which went before. The capital's fleet of four-wheeled 'growlers' and Hansom cabs, which alone drew on a total of 20,000 horses, now clearly felt the challenge of the piston engine. The motor omnibuses were superseding the horse-buses. The rich had their motor landaus, with a uniformed chauffeur in peaked cap and leather leggings, who sat up in front exposed to all weathers, just as coachmen had always done. The cars of the period, with their shining brasswork, huge acetylene lamps and meticulously painted coach-work, are today rightly recognised as individual works of art. The best were made in the heart of the West End.

These 'motors' were joined on the streets of London by electric trams, which had a spectacular tunnel of their own, starting from the Embankment and emerging in the middle of Kingsway, a new street named after Edward VII. Kingsway also made possible the linking of the LCC northern and southern tram systems. This was to be the last major improvement in central London until the Hyde Park boulevard was built in 1962. Kingsway is still largely lined with the prestige office blocks of the period, Africa House being perhaps the most resplendent example.

The king was a great francophile, and delighted to encourage his ministers in the settling of diplomatic differences between England and France—a policy which success- fully led to the 'Entente Cordiale' in 1904. As if reflecting this new London-Paris axis, the Ritz Hotel went up in Piccadilly, the joint work of French and British architects,

Mewès and Davis. There is no better evocation of rare Edwardian elegance than the interiors of the Ritz. In 1908 came the Franco-British Exhibition at the White City; the Central Line tube (opened by the king when he was Prince of Wales in 1900) was specially extended for the tremendous number of visitors.

England and France went into informal alliance because of the danger from Germany. In 1906, the Kaiser announced plans for a large number of cruisers. Seen from the Admiralty, these could only be designed to prey on our commerce. And the Germans also began to build their reply to the British super-battleship, the 'Dreadnought'. The naval building race between the two powers was now impossible to stop.

At the Court of St James, the royal levées, morning parties for men, became an increasingly feverish centre for intrigue and the picking up of significant gossip to be relayed back to the chancelleries of Europe. What would Britain really do if a general war broke out? Would she support France, or be a neutral?

The British politicians attended the levées in all the panoply of Court Dress or in the Privy Council uniform if they were members of it—white knee breeches, gold-embroidered coat, feather-fringed cocked hat and court sword. Their wives and daughters attended the court of King Edward and Queen Alexandra with ostrich feathers in their hair and trains to their long dresses, as prescribed by the Lord Chamberlain's regulations. Their necks and shoulders were white and plump, expanses of soft-scented flesh on which warm jewels sparkled. The figure aimed for was the 'hour-glass', with a tiny waist, an ample, monolithic bust and a balancing *derrière*.

In December 1905 Balfour's Conservative government had resigned, and the Liberals under Campbell-Bannerman formed an administration, pending an election. In January came a landslide victory for the Liberals. The whole previous pattern of politics now collapsed. Included in the huge anti-Conservative majority were thirty MPs elected under the label of Labour, and they came together formally in 1906 to create the Labour Party. Three of them were from London constituencies: West Ham, Woolwich and Deptford.

Conditions in the working class areas of the capital were still pitiful, even though London since 1888 had at least been administered by one central authority, the London County Council. The LCC had appointed a full-time medical officer in 1902, and his first report spoke of a large percentage of children with heads 'encrusted with scabs, exudation and lice'. Ringworm and favus (a particularly revolting scalp disease) also lurked in children's hair, their skins were disfigured by impetigo, and dental caries, ophthalmia and malnutrition were commonplaces of a child's life. The LCC cleared a few slums and put up replacement blocks, but hampered by lack of funds and of statutory powers, it was unable to do much more. Up to 1919 it had built 6,000 houses, mostly as replacements in slum areas, and a further 4,000 in new estates away from the centre; the first land for such schemes had been acquired in 1900 at Tooting.

This policy had been fostered by the Progressive Party, the Liberals in their London local government disguise. But as so often in the history of London's own government, in the local election of 1907 there was a big swing against the party in power at Westminster, and the Municipal Reform party (the Conservatives) captured the LCC, which they were to hold for the next quarter of a century. One of the big issues of the election had been the paddle-steamer service on the Thames, which the Progressives had started in 1905 as a regular public transport service (there were thirty steamers altogether). Engine breakdowns and collisions were frequent, and the new administration brought it to an end. Only Greenwich pier remains as a legacy.

In other spheres, however, transport in London was pushing ahead to give one of the best systems of any capital in the world. We have already mentioned the Kingsway tram tunnel. The tram network, electrified between 1901 and 1915, spread rapidly at the same time, reaching out as far as Barnet and Waltham Cross to the north, Uxbridge to the west, Chadwell Heath to the east and Purley to the south. The trams were thought of as the working man's transport. They started running much earlier than the buses, and their wider platforms were better suited to carry tools and so on. The London General Omnibus Company responded by introducing more and more motor buses (solid-tyred); their last horse bus was withdrawn in 1911.

Consolidation of the London transport system was rapidly taking place. In 1912 the London General bus company joined with the Underground Electric Railways Company, which had built or now controlled most of the tube system. The new group also controlled the principal privately owned tramways. The biggest tram network was however the LCC's municipally operated system.

This was the time of the tube. Apart from the Victorian Inner Circle (which mostly runs in a giant covered trench, rather than a tunnel), London had only two deep underground railways before 1906, the middle section of the present day Central line and three miles between Stockwell and the Monument. Then came C. T. Yerkes, an American financier. He put the Underground company together, and almost simultaneously the Bakerloo, the Piccadilly and the Hampstead and Highgate tunnels began to bore their way through the clay north of the river. (One reason why tubes did not expand south of the Thames was that the soil there, often wet gravel, presented great engineering problems.) The first two lines were opened in 1906, and the last, ending at Golders Green, in 1907.

Yerkes had decided to push on to Golders Green, then green fields and open country, as his American experience had shown that people followed the railway, and speculative building would attract traffic. He proved completely correct. But a development that turned out even more significant for London in the twentieth century is the 'garden suburb' laid out close to the station. Operating as a Trust under an Act of Parliament, the venture was not principally commercial, but designed to create an 'old world', restful atmosphere, like a country village with picturesque closes and greens. The estate was laid out by Raymond Unwin and Sir Edwin Lutyens (who also designed the churches and public buildings around the suburb's central square). The pleasant effect produced was to influence profoundly subsequent housing developments in London. Both private and LCC estates drew upon the Hampstead Garden Suburb for inspiration in the great housing expansion which followed the

First World War. After the suburb had shown the way, brown-brick terraces were replaced as the norm of London's housing by rows of semi-detached villas.

In the period 1901–14 however, London was becoming a much overcrowded place. The Victorian building boom had slowed down, and the high unemployment figures in the building industry at the time tell their own story. This recession had its counterpart in other industries, and unemployment in London became relatively more serious than elsewhere in the country. In 1904 the London Unemployed Fund was set up; it provided a model for an Act on a national scale the following year. The Liberal government's provision of some basic social security for the worker had its roots in very real distress, as did the industrial action launched by the Trade Unions—particularly the national railway strike in 1911, and the miners' strike the following year. The London dockers were also able, by strike action, to raise their 'tanner' an hour up to eightpence.

In Parliament, the last great classic clash of old and new divided not only MPs but the nation as well. To pay for the reforms, a 'People's Budget' had been introduced by Lloyd George, the Chancellor of the Exchequer. This the Lords threw out— an unheard of event, as financial bills were supposed to be sacrosanct. 'Ll. G.' carried the fight to the people. In a speech at Limehouse he attacked the hereditary principle: 'A fully-equipped duke costs as much to keep up as two "Dreadnoughts" and dukes are as great a terror, and last longer.'

The Liberals dissolved Parliament, and in January 1910 they were again returned to power. They considered this a mandate for a comprehensive social reform. In the middle of the approaching crisis, King Edward died, to be succeeded by George V, a re-incarnation of Queen Victoria in his domestic virtues, and stricter even than she in putting public duty before private cares. After a further election in December, the king promised the Liberal premier, Asquith, that he would create enough Liberal peers to swamp the Lords if they threw out the Parliament Bill, which would forever abolish their veto over legislation and only allow them powers of delay. The hot London summer was tense—the stench of the polluted Thames could be smelt all over the Palace of Westminster—but the peers gave in, though they fought to the last ditch.

No wonder that Britain's enemies reckoned that at last her social fabric was about to crack. Her cabinet ministers were pursued by suffragettes, women who chained themselves to the railings of Downing Street, and went cheerfully to Holloway Prison, to be degraded by forcible feeding when they went on hunger strikes.

The theatre reflected the questioning of social attitudes, particularly in the works of Bernard Shaw and John Galsworthy. But the West End musical stage sparkled with light-hearted musical comedies, which were very much home-grown. The great impresario, George Edwardes, with his internationally famous Gaiety Girls, many of whom really did marry into the oldest aristocracy, put on a succession of works by Lionel Monckton, like *The Quaker Girl*, *The Arcadians* and *Our Miss Gibbs*.

This was the apogee too of the British music hall. The houses increased both in number and in the size and standard of their accommodation. George Robey, Marie Lloyd and Vesta Tilly played to packed audiences, magnetic stars whose songs, mannerisms and catch-phrases were often on the nation's lips. But from 1905 the 'bioscope', the cinema, was a growing challenge. In 1911, the 94 cinemas of the County of London could seat three-quarters of the number of the music halls. Many films already were produced in Hollywood, but London made its own films at studios at Shepherd's Bush and Islington, and was the centre of the British industry. Dancing was taking a different turn; rag-time was coming in from across the Atlantic, and the slightly sinister tango (from South America) was danced at 'tango teas'.

The last prewar season at Covent Garden was one of unprecedented splendour. Among the works performed was Richard Strauss's *Der Rosenkavalier*, a loving evocation of the Vienna of the mid-eighteenth century. It turned out to be a requiem, not only for the Hapsburg Empire, but for the young men of the London season, who waltzed in Society's ballrooms to its languid tunes and all too soon were to be decimated by machine guns at the front.

L.S.&.P.C^o.

13

The Olympic Games of 1908, held at the White City, were a great triumph for Britain—and her mainly 'gentleman' athletes—who piled up three times as many points as the next competitor, the United States. The marathon was, however, one event which Britain did not win. First at the tape was the Italian Pietro Dorandi (above), but because he had collapsed and been revived before completing the race, he was disqualified. The second runner to finish the course, J. J. Hayes (USA), was declared the winner. Right, American athletes carry the victorious Hayes and his trophy through the stadium.

Before the 1914-18 war, cars were owned only by the rich
and mainly driven by chauffeurs, in imitation of the
coachmen they replaced. However, commercial vehicles were
also made by the early motor manufacturers. Above, two
Daimler products at the Commercial Motor Parade in 1913.
Right, two of the petrol-driven buses which gradually
replaced the horse buses (the last was withdrawn in 1911).
Motor buses, particularly welcome in central London where
there was no tram service, combined with the underground
to make the city's transport system one of the most efficient
(and expensive) in the world.

Poverty was the great social scourge before the 1914-18 war, as unemployment was after it. Lowly paid unskilled labourers in towns were particularly hard hit, especially in London, where rents were high and housing was short. Like the East End women, *right*, many families lived in appallingly cramped and sordid surroundings. Not surprisingly, children from such homes were often hungry: *above*, slum children crowd hopefully around a baker's cart. The lot of the urban poor improved after the strikes of 1911-12, which gained a rise for the worst-paid workers.

Right, a scene outside the Kensington branch of the
Women's Social and Political Union, a suffragist
organisation originally founded in Manchester in 1903 by
Mrs Emmeline Pankhurst. Above, Mrs Pankhurst and her
daughter Christabel (a rabidly militant campaigner)
outside Bow Street Magistrates' Court in 1908. Although
the suffragettes campaigned persistently until the war (and,
as so often, damaged their cause by their persistence),
women—and only those over 30—were not given the vote
until after the war. The 'flappers' (girls under 30) had to
wait until 1928.

Suffragettes advertised their campaign by means that have
become the archetypes of political protest: defiant
acceptance of imprisonment (and later forcible feeding) and
increasingly disruptive demonstrations. Overleaf, an
episode during the movement's later, more anarchic phase:
women demonstrators are led away after a march on
Buckingham Palace in 1914.

Above, King George V and Queen Mary riding in their Coronation procession in 1911; right, noble members of the congregation outside Westminster Abbey. In the same year, both king and peers were involved in a titanic constitutional struggle over the legislative powers of the House of Lords (precipitated by their refusal to pass Lloyd George's 'liberal' Budget of 1909). Their right of veto was eventually abolished by the Parliament Act 1911, passed by the Lords only after the king's assurance to Asquith that he would, if necessary, create enough Liberal peers to swamp the Die-hards' majority.

The War to end War

Immediately war was declared on Germany, the machinery which had been in long preparation swung into action. From the Admiralty's wireless masts in the heart of Whitehall, Winston Churchill, as First Lord, had ordered the fleet to sea as a precautionary measure. Now the signal was sent: 'Commence hostilities against Germany.' The tiny British Army went to Belgium, there to assist in the vain attempt to prevent the Germans overrunning the country. The Bank of England and the City put themselves in readiness to raise the finance required for the war; and Fleet Street (particularly, of course, the leading popular paper, Lord Northcliffe's *Daily Mail*) began to lash the civil population into a great wave of hatred for the Germans and all their works. They were aided in this by reports of a steady stream of German atrocities in Belgium, as the allied armies were rolled back.

Fashionable ladies had their dachshunds put down. The German bands, for long a cheerful feature of the London streets, disappeared as the players were rounded up and thrust into internment camps. Public parks and gardens—including Alexandra Palace—were disfigured with temporary buildings to accommodate these unfortunates, and soon a stream of refugees from Belgium to London had to be similarly housed.

Soon too, the requirements of government—war always seems to be good for bureaucrats—turned aristocrats out of their mansions, clubmen out of St James's and commercial travellers out of their favourite hotels. At first these expansions of the Civil Service were only expected to deal with the greatly increased requirements of the armed services, but as the concept of total war, and the mobilisation of civilian resources, became generally accepted, new ministries—Transport, Pensions, Labour and Shipping—were brought into existence, in many cases to continue, perhaps under different names and groupings, after the war had been won. The hotels in Northumberland Avenue, taken over in 1914, have remained government offices ever since.

Life became considerably drabber. The boat race, cricket test matches, these were abandoned until after the war. The British Museum closed. So did the Wallace collection, the Tate and most of the Victoria and Albert Museum. All the ceremonial uniforms of the Guards were immediately replaced by khaki.

Yet when the troops in the trenches sang 'Take me back to dear old Blighty', it wa
to the lights of London, to the dance halls, above all to the theatres that they—an
the officers in particular—looked. The all-time hit in the war years was *Chu Chin Chow*
Frederick Norton's oriental extravaganza, with its belly dancers ('more navel tha
millinery,' was one comment on this musical), closely followed by the *Maid of th*
Mountains. Escapist, lavishly staged with beautiful girls, they were what the boys fror
the Front wanted to see.

Transport was considerably curtailed. There were not nearly as many buses. Man
of them had in fact been taken over by the army in France, and used to bring up re
inforcements to the front. Cabs were very much scarcer, and the use of cab whistle
('one blast for a taxi, two for a hansom, three for a four-wheeler') was forbidden, a
the police used their whistles as an air-raid warning. Private motoring too was cut b
the petrol shortage, but the underground ran as usual, as did the trams. Now womer
proved their worth, as the suffragettes always said they would. They were conductor
on the underground, and on the buses and trams. They also worked in the new munitior
and aircraft factories set up—particularly in the Cricklewood area—to feed th
insatiable demand for the weapons of war.

The war did at least give the government the confidence that it could do things
that it could act effectively, and that things need no longer be left to private agencies
Important for London's health was the London and Home Counties Venereal Disease
Scheme in 1917, which not only checked the increase of such diseases, inevitable ir
time of war, but kept a check on them in the years to come. The Housing Act (1919)
gave the LCC the power at last to embark on a giant programme of housing London'
people, something even more necessary now that the nation had emerged from the
war with almost universal suffrage; with a few exceptions, all women over 30 and al
men over 21 now had the vote. The war had acted as catalyst, and in every directior
change had speeded up.

Right, new recruits taking the oath at the White City.

The recruitment drive was boosted by marches and meetings where speakers (often women) harangued the crowd with an extravagant mixture of jingoism and anti-German propaganda. Below right, a recruiting meeting in 1915 and, far right, a recruiting march by the King's Royal Rifle Corps.

No coal for the families, above, during the winter of 1917.
Fuel and clothes were in short supply in wartime, but on the
whole Londoners (and other civilians) suffered little
hardship—and much less injury—than they did during the
second war. *Right*, 'Dig for Victory' 1916 style—*growing
vegetables on a Dulwich allotment. The Ministry of Food
was one of five departments set up by Lloyd George for the
organisation of the war effort. Ration books were
introduced only in February 1918, but these had little
relevance to the supply of food, which was plentiful.

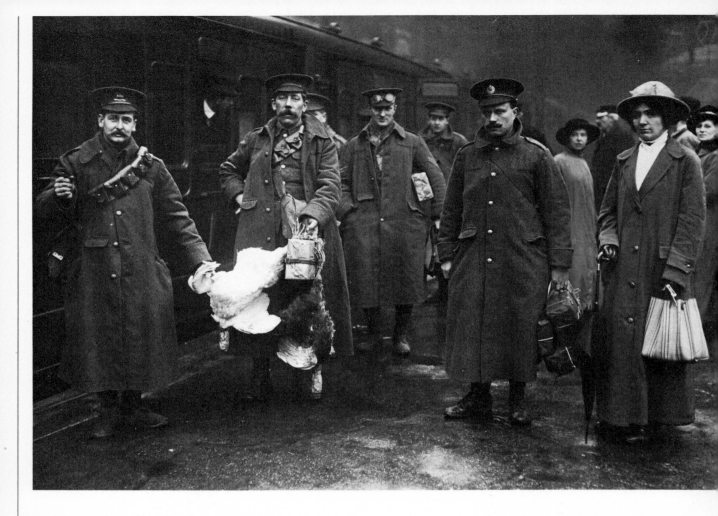

*Above, 'Tommies' leave for the front from Victoria Station,
carrying a few home comforts. On arrival in France troops
faced the horrors of trench warfare: acute danger and
discomfort and almost total military deadlock. The losses
were gigantic, particularly among junior officers, whose
casualties were three times greater than those of the 'other
ranks'. Right, ambulances carry wounded to the Charing
Cross Hospital in 1914.*

In April 1915 London experienced its first Zeppelin attack.
Right, bomb damage in Farringdon Street. The vulnerable
Zeppelins were soon superseded by aeroplanes, and the
German raids continued: they caused great excitement but
little damage. Above, a car patrols with a warning notice
to take cover during an expected air raid.

*Anti-German feeling during the war was often hysterical—
and deliberately provoked. Above, a shopkeeper proclaims
himself to be Russian to protect himself during anti-German
riots in the East End, often mistakenly directed at East
European Jewish immigrants.*

Right, the queue for the last night of Chu Chin Chow *in
July 1921. Frederick Norton's musical play was the great
hit of the war, crowded out every night by soldiers on leave
from France.*

The wartime shortage of manpower was partly overcome by
employing women, who demanded (in the words of Mrs
Pankhurst) 'the right to serve'. Many, like the girls in the
lens factory, right, and the women porters, above, took on
what had been considered to be exclusively man's work—
jobs that reverted to men when the war was over. Other gaps
left by the war—such as low-grade jobs in shops and offices
—fell permanently to women.

Above, a procession passing the Cenotaph on Victory Day
1919—a later and more sober celebration of peace than
Armistice Day itself. The Cenotaph was designed by Sir
Edwin Lutyens and put up in wood for the first anniversary
of Armistice Day. The Glorious Dead it commemorated
numbered half a million from Britain and nearly a quarter
of a million from the Empire.

Right, scenes of rejoicing in London on Armistice Day,
November 11, 1918. The end of war was riotously greeted
by Londoners (the police turned a more-or-less blind eye), of
whom the chief revellers were troops from the Dominions.
The troops at the front, in contrast, had little chance to
celebrate the end of four years of terrible war.

The modern movement in architecture had few disciples in England, in contrast to its widespread practice and acceptance on the Continent. A rare and astonishingly advanced example is Peter Jones in Sloane Square (1936). Note the exciting way in which the elegant glass curtain curves around the corner into Kings Road.

The Face of London

If architecture is frozen music, then the best of London's Edwardian buildings are Elgar: huge, swelling, imperial. It was only as the British Empire began to be challenged by new young giants that anything substantial began to be done to create an imperial capital. The Victorians perhaps had been too busy making money and carving out bits of Africa. Now it was their successors who called (in a very small way, it must be admitted, looking at Vienna and Paris) art to the aid of Empire.

A triumphal way was needed, to connect Buckingham Palace, where lived the crowned symbol of the Empire, and the centre of government. So the Mall, a pleasant and slightly rural *allée* running alongside St James's Park, was converted. It was widened, and at one end, in front of Buckingham Palace, a circular and grandiose memorial to Queen Victoria was erected in the decade which followed her death, though in a very bosomy, *beaux arts* manner. The queen, surely, would have preferred something gothic, like dear Albert's own memorial. Also perpetuating the queen's memory was Admiralty Arch, at the other end of the Mall. By Sir Aston Webb (who also refaced Buckingham Palace at about the same time), it provides accommodation for the Admiralty, including a magnificent flat for the First Sea Lord.

Sir Aston used the classical manner, with columns—usually attached—*ad lib*. He was none the less considerably more restrained than some of his contemporaries, as the merest glance upwards at Norman Shaw's Piccadilly Hotel will reveal. Here is a screen of enormous tuscan columns, perched high above the street, as if Piranesi had placed them there. This building, which dates from 1905, began the fashion for inflated scale in this part of London, under the influence of which Nash's Regent Street, humanly proportioned in yellow stucco, was demolished between this time and the 1920s. In Piccadilly Circus, the County Fire Office (1925) was given great stone arches; at Oxford Circus, Sir Henry Tanner provided a design which was repeated four times at different dates between 1913 and the end of the 1920s, until the four sides were symmetrically complete. So academic is this arrangement that it is quite without impact.

45

For even though called upon to provide imperial touches, the Edwardian architects could not but be affected by the spirit of the age. Too many of them were far more gentlemanly than any artist should ever be. They were torn between a code of good manners and the florid nature of their time. Kingsway, a development of the time, and its office buildings, have already been mentioned in Section One. At its foot is the semicircular sweep of Aldwych, and here can be seen one or two buildings which are shamelessly and gloriously uninhibited. The Waldorf Hotel (1907–8) has a lively façade, which tiers up like a wedding cake, complete with cherubs. Australia House (begun 1912, completed 1918) has the most three-dimensional elevation of any building in London—great groups of statuary, in stone, bronze and other materials are writhing to get free. This is Edwardian baroque, at its vulgar, optimistic best. So also is the Selfridge's building in Oxford Street (partly designed by Daniel Burnham, an American from Chicago).

It was odd that Norman Shaw turned to monumentalism in the Piccadilly Hotel, for he had pioneered the domestic style of the late Victorian age. Perhaps it is to his credit that he rose to the need now for larger blocks of building with something unexpected. But on the continent of Europe they were responding in an entirely different way, exploiting new materials, particularly concrete, and the plastic possibilities it brings, and experimenting both with the sinuous shapes of *art nouveau* and with the severe forms of early functionalism. All this was largely to pass London by. Only one architect was able to make its influence felt in his buildings. This was Charles Holden, whose British Medical Association Building in the Strand (now Rhodesia House) of 1907 was a solitary example. It caused an outrage because of Epstein's naked figures on its façade; the BMA caved in, and had the genitals of the statues mutilated, and the faces too, for good measure.

Let us leave the last flourishes of the Edwardians with an example which has other interest besides the architectural: Cockspur Street, off Trafalgar Square. Here the ocean liner companies established their headquarters, and so lucrative was their business, that up went prestige office blocks to give a land-based impression of the luxuries they offered afloat. The whole street has something of the atmosphere of the *Titanic*. Particularly good for evoking such reveries are the P. & O. building of 1907, the French Line, Oceanic House and Aston Webb's building for the Canadian National Railways.

London's public architecture in the years from the Edwardians to the final emergence of the international style in our own time suffered from a double disaster. This was the work of Sir Edwin Lutyens and Sir Herbert Baker. Practically every major building in the 1920s and 1930s went to this couple, who were great friends from the time they were both pupils in the same office. Their buildings are soulless, bland, yet in a curious way ingenious, but not ever enough to erase the stupefying good taste which pervades them. Utterly unexciting, completely in accord with the taste of the middle-class mediocrities who ruled England between the wars, they are in truth the monuments of the men of Munich.

Lutyens had begun by designing pleasant country houses in the tradition established in the 1860s by William Morris and Philip Webb. His first major London building was the Country Life office in Tavistock Street (1904). From this he steadily advanced, playing an important part, as we have seen, in the laying out of Hampstead Garden suburb, designing some of its houses and its public buildings. But he soon moved forward to monumentalism (though he continued to design expensive country houses for millionaire clients). The Cenotaph, Whitehall, is also his. It was first put up as a temporary structure in wood for the first Armistice commemoration in 1919, but soon was replaced in Portland stone.

Lutyens was awarded the most important commission in the British Empire, the planning and the design of the principal buildings of the new capital of India, New Delhi. He had however time for Britannic House in Finsbury Circus, for the elevation of Terminal House, Grosvenor Gardens, and several Midland Banks, including the great head office in the Poultry (built between 1924 and 1939) and a generally admired example in an accurate pastiche of Christopher Wren in Piccadilly. This last is at least well-mannered, for it is on the corner of Wren's own St James's church. Lutyens rebuilt Middle Temple Hall, and in 1935, the new grand headquarters for Reuter's in Fleet Street. He was known for his variations in the style of the great British seventeenth-century master—'Wrenaissance', as it was often called. He also introduced a trick to his elevations which was to be copied by many other architects in the inter-war period. This was the device of designing what was basically a classical building with an enriched ground floor—rusticated stone work, porticos, elaborate framing to the windows—and then thrusting in perhaps eight tiers of plain windows (as many as the restrictions on the height of buildings in London would allow) until the topmost floor, when again the classical mode took over.

This unpleasant compromise became the hallmark of 'banker's Georgian'. And no one used it more than Sir Herbert Baker. Lutyens could produce something harmonious, and he was certainly respectful of past work. Baker was not. After qualifying, he had established his practice in South Africa, and something of the ruthlessness of the Boer seemed to have entered into his system. (He was always considered to be South Africa's own, for he was commissioned to put up the Parliament buildings in Pretoria, and was the natural choice for South Africa House in Trafalgar Square.)

In 1921 Baker was commissioned to expand the Bank of England, designed by Soane in 1788. Baker burrowed industriously, and erected his own quirky temple rising out of Soane's strong encircling wall. Nasty, fussy sculptures with hidden significances, by Charles Wheeler, were ordered by Baker. Most of his buildings have these coy little items. Other Baker buildings are India House in Aldwych, the Royal Commonwealth Society in Northumberland Avenue, Church House, Westminster, Electra House on the Embankment, and London House, an enormous hall of residence for Commonwealth students in Bloomsbury.

Only a few buildings stand out in the London of 1910–30. Among them, the Michelin garage of 1910 on the Old Brompton Road evokes the spirit of early motoring perfectly. The building, though perfectly fitting its function, has the most amusing touches of *art nouveau* about it, including tiled pictures of the great motoring events of the period. Indeed, it is to industrial structures that we have to look for any visual excitement or amusement. The 1920s style really blossoms along the Great West Road, where the Firestone, Coty and Gillette factories, with their jazz and colour embellishments, complex *art deco* entrances, merit a close look. In central London, seek out Ideal House in Great Marlborough Street, behind the London Palladium. Faced entirely in black marble, abstract jazz patterns in gold and red ornament the windows and doors. It was designed by the American architect Raymond Hood, and built in 1928.

Polite buildings which are in the modern style are few, but Heal's (1916) in the Tottenham Court Road is worth noticing. What is now the headquarters of London Transport, 55 Broadway, St James's, is not handsome, but it has, even today, an interesting brutal quality, and it shows off well some splendid sculptures. It was designed by Charles Holden, and put up in the late twenties.

With the 1930s, new building in London really got under way. The capital had become the centre of light industry, the car had finally made its impact on the townscape (with circular and arterial roads now adding to the existing network). Because of the motor car, London was expanding, not only along the railway lines, but to distances beyond and between them. One of the signs of this new primacy of the roads even for long-distance travel was the Victoria Coach Station (1931). Charles Holden now produced some of his most striking buildings for the expanded Piccadilly Line with his stations at Arnos Grove and Cockfosters. The newly boosted demand for more electricity resulted in Battersea Power Station, a design of immense strength by Sir Giles Gilbert Scott.

The destruction of the old mansions on Park Lane continued. They were replaced by giant luxury hotels, in which such famous bands as Ambrose played. The hotel which most successfully captures the spirit of its period is the Dorchester. The dear

'Dorch', with its unchanged lettering and its splendid lifts is the most apt symbol of it
time, a palace fit for debs to dine in. Another monument of the period was the black
glass palace of the *Daily Express*, exactly hitting off the glamour which was such an
essential part of the paper under Lord Beaverbrook.

At last things were moving away from the Herbert Baker sterilities. A refugee from
totalitarian Europe, Lubetkin, put up blocks of flats in the most graceful and ultra-
modern manner at Highpoint, Highgate. Stores like Barkers of Kensington (delight-
fully 'futuristic'—reminiscent of the probing searchlights of the 20th Century Fox
symbol, which flashed nightly on the screens of a thousand Odeons, Gaumonts, Ritzes
and Regals in the London area) and Peter Jones in Sloane Square (a very advanced
design, with a subtle use of curtain walling) and HMV in Oxford Street were breaking
utterly with pomposity. One or two experimental villas, like 66 Frognal (by Connell,
Ward and Lucas) and the Sun House (by Maxwell Fry) just down the road, also made
their appearance.

Even the public bodies acknowledged the new trend. The Westminster City
Council's Central Cleansing and Transport Department of 1938 is a model, and the
Gas Light and Coke Company built subsidised housing for its workers in Ladbroke
Grove to the design of Maxwell Fry. The new airways corporation, BOAC, opened its
Victoria terminal in 1939, with traces of both the old and the new architecture. At its
rear, the trains slid out of their special platform, taking passengers to Southampton
and the great flying boats of the Empire service. New Town Halls in East London, at
Dagenham, Hornsey and Greenwich, owed little to previous ideas of municipal
architecture.

A new Waterloo bridge had been sanctioned, and designed by Sir Giles Gilbert
Scott in 1939. But now war was to intervene, and Waterloo Bridge was not to be
completed until 1945. A significant indication of what London was to endure now
appeared on Horse Guards Parade—the Admiralty Citadel. It was the first fortification
to be built in London since the Civil War of the 1640s.

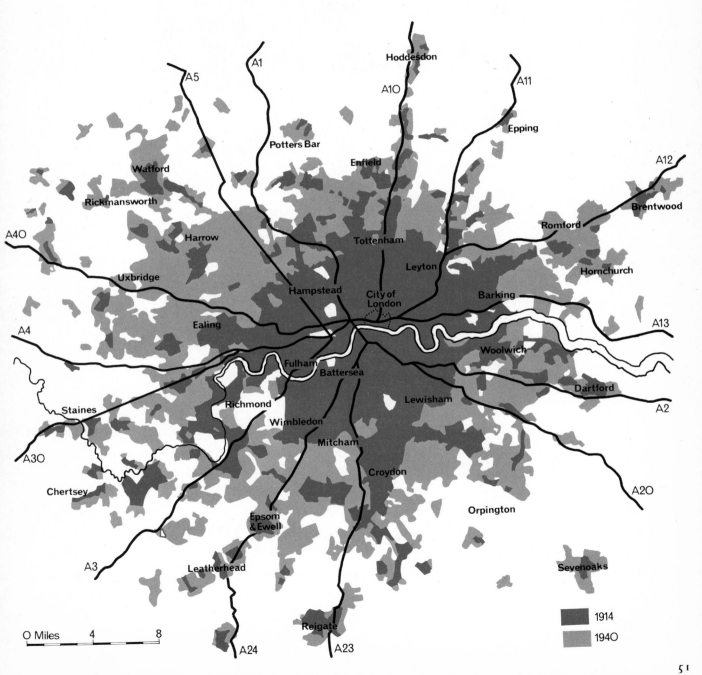

Hoddesdon

A5

A1

A11

A10

Potters Bar

Epping

Enfield

A12

Watford

Brentwood

Rickmansworth

Romford

A40

Harrow

Tottenham

Hornchurch

Uxbridge

Leyton

Hampstead

Barking

City of London

A13

Ealing

A4

Woolwich

Fulham

Battersea

Dartford

Richmond

Lewisham

A2

Wimbledon

Staines

Mitcham

A30

Croydon

A20

Chertsey

Orpington

Epsom & Ewell

Sevenoaks

A3

Leatherhead

1914

1940

O Miles   4   8

Reigate

A24

A23

Many interwar buildings —particularly cinemas and factories—were decorated with jazz or 'modernistic' motifs, usually totally unrelated to the actual design of the building. *Right*, the elaborately patterned entrance to the Hoover Factory (1937) in West London. *Far right*, a view of the ceiling at Dagenham Town Hall (1938), decorated with an interlocking pattern that is typical of the time.

Two exercises in public building. Right, Broadcasting House (1931), an ungraceful mass with particularly ugly windows, though it is perhaps slightly redeemed by a fine sculpture by Eric Gill over the entrance. Rather more ponderous statuary also adorns Australia House (1918), far right, a neo-baroque monument to the unshaken imperialism of the Edwardian age.

A pioneer of the modern movement in Britain was
Lubetkin, who, like many avant-garde architects of the
time, was a refugee from Europe. One of his most popular
designs (with the Tecton group) was the Penguin Pool at
London Zoo (1934), above, a light-hearted and graceful
exercise in the use of reinforced concrete. A more serious
undertaking was the building of two blocks of flats in
Highgate. The high quality of the first, Highpoint 1, put
London on the architectural map; Highpoint 2 is less
distinguished and slightly confused by detail, notably a
pair of mock-serious Greek caryatids supporting the
entrance canopy (right).

The work of Sir Charles Holden covered a wide range of
time and styles. Above, Arnos Grove (1932), among his
most successful designs for underground stations—simple,
unpretentious and still fresh to the modern eye. Holden's
earlier work is severe, its uncompromising angular forms
London's sole evidence of the impact of early functionalism.
Right, the BMA Building (1907), now Rhodesia House, a
stark contrast to the palatial exuberance of Holden's
contemporaries. Epstein's statues flanking the second-floor
windows were also in advance of their time, and were
mutilated by public request.

Some of the most pleasing commercial buildings in London between the wars were those designed without too much thought for prestige or pretention. Two such buildings were produced by the age of motoring: above, Victoria Coach Station (1931), an example of the 'modernistic' use of a contrasting strong vertical (the tower) with low-lying horizontal wings; right, the Michelin Building (1910), remarkable for its art nouveau lettering and motifs.

Houses were built in large numbers on the outskirts of London after the 1914-18 war; these, if not quite 'homes for heroes', were a great improvement on the slums they replaced. Right, a view of the Becontree Estate, one of the largest; like most government-inspired housing schemes it was built in a simple, cottage style. Private clients chose more exotic houses, where decoration usually took second place to design. The luxurious example in the Bishop's Avenue, Highgate, above, is basically Georgian with French provincial touches.

Two pioneering essays in private housing. Right, the staircase at the Isokon flats in Hampstead (1934), an uncompromising gesture in support of the modern movement. The Sun House, Frognal (far right), a simple yet elegant design by Maxwell Fry (1935), is another worthy survivor from the period.

Norma and Constance Talmadge at a ball in 1922. Upper-class young women were beginning to become really emancipated, wearing shorter, skimpier and less constricting clothes and underclothes, using make-up and smoking and drinking in public.

The Jazz Age

The 1920s, which more often than not are today seen as the Jazz Age of the 'Bright Young Things', had in Britain both a grim and a gay side. By the end of the war, the country's mobilisation had become total. An unparalleled social discipline had been imposed on all ranks of society, and the Prime Minister, Lloyd George, had gathered into his own hands more power than any previous holder of his office.

With an enlarged electorate, and all the strains of war still bearing on the minds of the people, the election of 1919 was fought as an exercise in demagoguery. Trafalgar Square, scene of recruiting meetings during the war, now rang to cries of 'Make Germany Pay', and 'Homes Fit For Heroes'. The first proved to be an impossible undertaking, but the necessary legislation was put through to try to make the second an ultimate reality. The LCC responded, and immediately began the purchase of vast tracts of country outside its boundaries for entirely new estates for working people. Of these, Becontree became the largest municipal estate in the world, 2,800 acres in extent, with 500 reserved for playing fields and open spaces. The houses were laid out as attractively as possible, with architectural variations; some were faintly Georgian in flavour, others had a hint of Tudor. This was a pattern universally followed both in private and public housing estates in the interwar years, though some very rich developments strayed to a Hollywood Spanish Mission style, all green tiles and wrought iron, as in Bishop's Avenue, N.W.3.

The capital continued to grow as an area of industrial importance. By 1940, about a quarter of all the workers in England and Wales were employed in the London region. In that suburban ring which developed almost entirely between 1918 and 1939, all the new industries which supplied the necessities of the changed conditions of everyday life began to concentrate. The most important was the West London industrial belt. Here the ordnance factories were built during the war, and private industry took them over when they were no longer required by the government. At Park Royal, ordnance factories were also established, and after some delay light engineering moved in during the mid-1920s, and the area boomed between 1928 and 1935.

This West London manufacturing area runs from Cricklewood, taking in Wembley and Willesden, along the line of the North Circular Road, to Park Royal, North Acton and North Hammersmith. Here the belt throws out three westward spurs. Two follow the roads, one south-west along the Great West Road, continuing very patchily to Staines, and the other following the line of Western Avenue to Alperton, Perivale and Greenford. The third follows the GWR line to Southall and Hayes. What is interesting is that this manufacturing belt very largely makes things for use in the London area—bodies for London Transport buses, motor-car components for Fords at Dagenham, luxury goods for the West End market. The workers in these factories come either from the new suburban estates developed at the same time, or from further afield, since the great improvements in public and private transport meant that workers no longer needed to be crammed within walking distance of their jobs.

Another industrial belt of some importance, following yet another arterial road of the 1920s, the Great Cambridge Road, runs up the Lea Valley. Unlike the more engineering-based West London area, items of everyday use—electric light bulbs, shoes, stationery—have been made there since the twenties.

But the early twenties were not a time of unclouded economic prosperity. At times in 1919 strikes made life in London worse than in war time. Rationing was still in force, and the lights were dim because of a shortage of electricity; the railwaymen and even the police at one point, came out on strike. The strains of adjustment to a new economic situation continued through the decade, rising to a climax in the General Strike of 1926.

This was seen at the time as the nearest that Britain had been to revolution for almost a century. The government, which had assumed full emergency powers, appealed to the public to volunteer to run essential services, and the middle classes responded with glee. It was such a lark, they felt, to drive buses and trains, to unload essential supplies; titled ladies acted as stable lads to the dear GWR dray horses at Paddington, or ladled out soup to their fellow workers on the job. In came armoured cars, to protect convoys of foodstuff on their way to the markets. The government issued its own newspaper, edited by Winston Churchill, a Cabinet Minister. The TUC, from its Headquarters in Eccleston Square, also had its mouthpiece, *The British Worker*. But in spite of what the more extreme government supporters thought, the TUC was really most concerned to end the whole thing amicably, and, if anything, feared the Bolsheviks even more than Mr Baldwin, the Prime Minister, did. The strike ended, in the south of England at least, without recrimination.

From then onwards, the country became more and more two nations, the old heavy-industrial areas getting increasingly depressed, while consumer-goods orientated London prospered. Social life in the West End, with 'bottle-parties' (at which one paid heavily for one's bottle) and a mushroom growth of night-clubs, was (if the popular papers were to be believed) notorious for drugs and drunkenness. The 'Night-Club Queen' was Mrs Meyrick, who opened the first of a succession of clubs, 'The 43', in 1921. A Lancashire millionaire brought her six Daimler-loads of showgirls one night for a champagne party, and her members included foreign royalty and show people. The dancing was wild, and went on all night. The steps were the jerky, frenetic ones which characterised the 1920s, but much of the music has proved immortal, and the tunes which were first played then are always being revived. Numbers which were also dances in their own right included the 'Charleston' and the 'Black Bottom'.

Those who had neither the money nor the taste for such expensive pleasures now had the opportunity to 'listen in'. For broadcasting had arrived, with the London station 2 LO, having its studios at Savoy Hill. The British Broadcasting Company was formed by wireless-set manufacturers, so that people would at least have something to listen to when they bought radios. But they chose a strange, idealistic General Manager, John Reith, who rapidly developed the idea of public service broadcasting, which was later embodied in the Corporation. He had managed to preserve a measure of independence for the BBC even at the time of the General Strike. As the newspapers became

more and more sensationalist, people looked to the BBC for reliable news, as well a
for music and educational broadcasts.

The drone of aircraft engines began to be heard increasingly over London, for ai
travel had arrived, particularly for trips to Paris and Amsterdam. From Hendon, an
then from Croydon, the great Handley Page biplanes lumbered over the grass runway
and set off to Paris at the stately speed of 90 mph.

Flying, because of its cost, was only for the rich and sophisticated. For them, life
freed now from most of the social restrictions and inhibitions of prewar times, coul
be immensely attractive. The London theatre of the twenties both provided a
amusement for this class and accurately mirrored their life, particularly in many of th
plays of Noël Coward, who cleverly projected himself as the epitome of Londo
urbanity. In 1929 the talkies came to London, and soon afterwards the people of th
suburbs were able to stroll along twice weekly to their local cinema, there to enjo
the golden voices of Jeanette MacDonald and Maurice Chevalier, sweet symbols of th
international nature of this entertainment.

Writers on their part now tried to write frankly about sex. D. H. Lawrence ha
his poems seized (and an exhibition of some rather bad paintings by him was raided an
closed). A novel with a lesbian theme, *The Well of Loneliness*, was banned. Leading thi
rearguard action was the perpetual Home Secretary of the 1920s, Sir William Joynson
Hicks, a strict Low Churchman. His brushes with everyone, from the literary lions to
Mrs Meyrick, provided constant public amusement.

Sir William (and even more his lady) did not like the short skirts and bobbed hai
which set the fashion of freedom for the women of the period. The Joynson-Hickse
preferred corsets. But the younger woman wore the minimum under her flimsy dress
She often achieved this by 'banting' to a boyish slimness, so that in fact there was ver
little that needed substantial support. The dangers of over-enthusiastic dieting apart
there was now an increasing emphasis on healthiness, which was to find its ultimate
expressions in the following decade.

The aftermath of war. Right, soldiers queue at a demobilisation
centre in Whitehall in 1919. At first, demobilisation was slow,
release depending on how important a man's civilian job was held to
be. Mutinies and demonstrations resulted among the disgruntled
troops, but their grievance vanished when Churchill, the secretary
for war, adopted the principle 'first in, first out'. Above, some of
a large party of disabled soldiers entertained to tea at Lyons Corner
House. A million and a half servicemen were permanently injured by
wounds or affected by gas.

Above, alternative transport during the Railway Strike,
1919, one of a wave of post-war industrial disputes. The
railwaymen struck against a threat to reduce their wages,
but their union managed to negotiate a rise. Trade Unions
were growing in power and membership, as was the
Parliamentary Labour Party, which gained 13 seats
between 1918 and 1922. In January 1924, Ramsay
MacDonald (right, with a group of supporters) became
the first Labour Prime Minister—and proved, if nothing
else, that socialists could dress and behave correctly at
formal gatherings.

Right, the front page of a brochure for the Empire Exhibition at Wembley, a vast 'expo' to which even the smallest colony made its contribution. The stadium and the empire pool survive as memorials to this imperial communion.

Far right, the new underground station at Piccadilly in 1928 with a battery of 'slot' machines for tickets. In 1929 the Underground carried 616 million passengers, and throughout the twenties its swift and efficient service, combined with the electrification of the railways, helped to create new dormitory towns far out in the Home Counties.

THE WONDERS of Wemble

64 Photos   HUMANI NIHIL A ME ALIENUM PURO   One Shilli

IN AID OF
The London Hospital
Founded 1740

Souvenir Guide to Lond

During the General Strike of 1926, middle-class volunteers—like the emergency train crew, right—kept essential services going. Though the strike was a genuine confrontation of the classes, there was little violence. Churchill, always belligerent, tried unsuccessfully to provoke conflict by parading armoured cars through the streets of London (below right). The strike ended after 10 days without winning any acceptable concession for the miners, whose grievances had precipitated the strike. Far right, a deputation of miners marching to London in 1927.

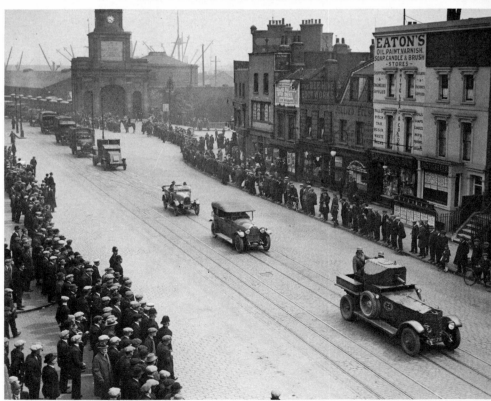

Far right, a cheap crystal set (wireless), costing only 7s 6d, seen at the British Wireless Exhibition at Olympia in 1924. Telecommunications had other uses: right, the control tower of Croydon Airport. From 1924 Imperial Airways ran regular flights to the Continent and to parts of the Empire. Below right, an Argosy airliner ready for its inaugural flight to India (in a week) in 1929.

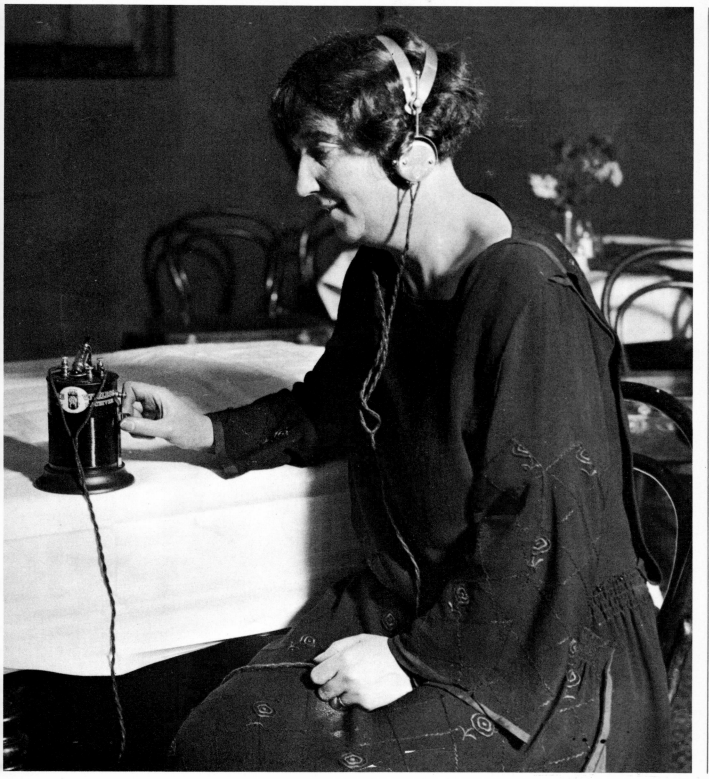

Dancing became the rage after the war. Starting with the
tango, the one-step and the hesitation waltz, dancers soon
graduated to the more frenetic rhythms of the Jazz Age.
Particularly popular were the American-imported
Charleston and the Black Bottom. Above, a group of
would-be experts in the Charleston. Another craze among
the more sophisticated was the frequenting of nightclubs, of
which the 'queen' was Mrs Kate Meyrick. Right, Mrs Meyrick
celebrating with friends her return from a spell in prison.
Like all night-club owners, she was always tangling with the
law over the licensing laws and her club status.

*Early rites in the worship of the motorcar. Above, a 'baby'
Morris, and, right, a Morris Major. To prosper, the motor
industry had to overcome its piecemeal, small-scale
beginnings: in 1923 there were 98 different manufacturers,
many producing single, hand-made models. By 1930, the
number of private cars had swollen to over a million and
60 per cent of the industry was controlled by two firms.*

Spectators of polo at Hurlingham (above) and racing at Ascot (right). Such occasions, which included Henley Regatta, the Eton and Harrow Match, were (as they are today) rallying points for the upper-middle class, then still firmly buttressed in their position of privilege by greatly superior wealth and education.

Harry Roy, one of the best-known band leaders of the thirties. A big band, usually with a resident crooner, was a feature of every luxury hotel, where every night there was dancing to its sweet, sentimental strains.

The Early Thirties

London entered the 1930s with all the outward signs of opulent prosperity. The fashionable world of socialites, with their clubs, parties and chic luxury flats, so well depicted in the early novels of Evelyn Waugh, stamped a brittle smartness on Mayfair and the West End. In 1929 a Labour Government had been returned, but the one-time revolutionary reformers had been largely tamed in the drawing rooms of the Establishment. The aitch-dropping J. H. Thomas loved evening clothes so much that he was depicted in cartoons as the 'Rt. Hon. Stuffed Shirt'. The premier, Ramsay Mac-Donald, was later to say, when he formed a National Government with leading Liberals and Conservatives, that every duchess in London would be rushing to kiss him. It would not be, for quite a number of them, the very first time.

The National Government was the response, in 1931, to the worst economic crisis of modern times. The Wall Street crash and the subsequent American depression spread across the sea to Europe. Unemployment rose. Then foreign financiers lost confidence in sterling, and rushed to withdraw their funds. A government of all the talents was considered, particularly by the king (monarchs are natural coalitionists), the only solution. Unfortunately, talent was very thin on the ground, and the two most able men in Parliament, Lloyd George and Churchill, were cold-shouldered by the Cabinet-makers.

A Means Test and a universal axing of government expenditure were decreed (together with Imperial Preference) as the medicine for recovery. Demonstrations against the cutting back were held in Parliament Square, and were charged down by the police. Trafalgar Square and the Albert Hall also were the venues of protest meetings; but the real hardship was in the provinces, and a National Hunger March was organised to converge on London. Thousands bore a petition, signed by a million people, to a rally in Hyde Park. Again the police charged. A hundred people were injured.

The distress and the seeming callousness of the government (the country's most brilliant economist, John Maynard Keynes, said that their policy was the opposite of what was required—money should be pumped into the economy, not taken out caused many young middle-class people to turn left-wing. Capitalism had, it seemed self-evident from the world-wide collapse, at last been proved a failure. At Oxford and Cambridge, people like Philby, Burgess and Maclean were sitting ducks for recruitment into the service of international communism. Brimming as they were with guilt for their life of privilege, they turned to what seemed to them the only alternative system. Many of the younger intellectuals were either communists or 'fellow-travellers'. They included the poets W. H. Auden, C. Day Lewis and Stephen Spender.

Another alternative to the problem of mass unemployment in an industrial society was offered after 1933—Nazism. Hitler's brand of Fascism took Mussolini's basic idea and added to it German thoroughness and fanaticism. (Italy had been Fascist for over ten years before Hitler came to power in Germany, but had showed no signs of racial intolerance or of upsetting international peace.) The Nazis systematically persecuted the Jews, and destroyed the fundamental rights of all men, particularly the intellectual freedoms. A terrible foreboding was now in the air.

But in Britain, and in prosperous London in particular, it seemed as if the mass of the people, still numbed from the 1914–18 War and astonished that the country had after all survived the economic difficulties of the 1920s, deliberately refused to face the awful possibilities of the future. They had been fed with the idea that the world had, more or less, disarmed, but still leaving the British Fleet as by far the largest in Europe. It was problematical whether Hitler came to power, or, if he did, what he would do. And so, in the period of five years between 1930 and 1935, the people of London and the surrounding area settled down to enjoy themselves in the new world which had suddenly come to fruition around them.

It was recognisably the world as we know it. There were many more cars, and they were plainly mass-produced, having now that pressed-out look about their bodies that they have today. A little car, an Austin Seven, a Ford 8 (which by 1935 could be had for £100), a Baby Morris, these were now within the reach of many a Londoner, ensconced with his family in their suburban semi. Plastic had come in for all sorts of domestic fixtures, like electric light switches. Bakelite, always either brown or black and with a characteristic smell of its own, was also used for the interior fittings of car dash-boards and even for the making of entire radio cabinets. Wireless sets were now no longer the collection of trailing wires, separate loud-speakers and other paraphernalia that they once had been, but, rationalised and domesticated, they sat in specially designed pieces of furniture in nearly everyone's sitting-room.

There was now an emphasis on popular, democratic enjoyment, more decorous than in the previous decade, with a gentle, corporate spirit. The bright young things had become young couples with families. Wild open-air parties which were reached by sports car were replaced by 'road houses' and by wholesome entertainment for all the family. A chumminess was in the air, epitomised in the songs of Gracie Fields, like 'Sally' (though she sang of a Lancashire remote from its depressed 1930s state), and the novels and plays of J. B. Priestley, particularly his best-seller *The Good Companions*. A sweeter, more sentimental kind of popular tune, many of them British, was broadcast by the BBC or was played on the gramophone. Henry Hall's band ('Teddy Bears' Picnic') was the most popular of all; it crossed the Atlantic with the *Queen Mary* on her maiden voyage in 1936. Vocalists with the bands affected a soft upper-class croon, perfectly elocuted. The national nightingale was London's own Jessie Matthews—she was born in Soho—who sang in just that way, but did much more. She starred in C. B. Cochran's West End shows, and in a series of successful musical films, where, in diaphanous draperies—as in the film *Evergreen*—she danced in a gracefully athletic style only too clearly derived from Miss Prunella Stack's exercises for the Women's League of Health and Beauty.

The cult of the body was now upon the land. Lidos were being opened all over London. The Labour Government constructed one in the Royal Parks, on the shores of the Serpentine. It was opened in June 1930 by George Lansbury, the popular First Commissioner of Works, who himself came from the East End, with a warning not to

95

write names on walls, or carve them in the woodwork. The trains of the GWR carryin
hopeful sun-bathers to the beaches of the West Country were now fitted with vitagla
windows so that none of the precious ultra-violet rays would be lost. And on Goo
Friday morning in 1932 a 'Hikers' Mystery Express' steamed out of Paddington full
haversacked Londoners travelling to some unknown country destination. The Souther
for its part ran 'Ramblers' Harvest Moon Specials' in the Home Counties. Spor
clothes were now summer leisure wear for both sexes, often in special fabrics lik
aertex, which were woven very loosely to 'allow the body to breathe'.

Dresses lengthened after 1930. Hats were floppy, and the ubiquitous cloche disa
peared. *Charmeuse* and *crepe-de-chine* were the fabrics of fashion, and synthetics lik
rayon came into their own. The effect aimed for was 'sheerness', particularly i
stockings of 'artificial silk'. Long legs were in. But in 1933 there was a softer revival
with muslin much used and the 'body line' came back. There was a distinct perio
quality about women's clothes now, helped by costume films. The Regency and th
eighteenth century were popular, crinolined dolls making telephone covers in th
bedrooms of the ladies of the richer suburbs. 'Old Vienna' was popularised by operet
and film. Isherwood's novel *Prater Violet* gives an amusing account of this vogue for th
Viennese. The best-dressed woman of 1934 was Princess Marina, whose wedding to th
Duke of Kent was the fashion event of the year.

Even Noël Coward followed the fashion for the Viennese with *Bitter Sweet*. But i
1931 he put life into patriotism, and filled the stage at Drury Lane with *Cavalcad*
which traced the story of a South London family from the Boer War to the time of i
presentation. Spectacular, needing huge lifts for its scenery, it was a far cry fro
Private Lives, with which he had begun the decade, a story of a brittle sophisticate
couple—played by Coward himself and Gertrude Lawrence—who, though divorce
and remarried, still hankered for each other. Such worldliness was rare; for mo
people, divorce was still a heavy social and moral stigma—as King Edward's supporter
found to their surprise in the coming abdication crisis.

The depression and its effects. Above, hunger marchers
from Dundee at Euston Station. Scotland was designated a
'special'—that is, a distressed—area in 1934, but little
was done to alleviate the chronic unemployment there.
Meantime, the financial crisis of 1931 led the National
Government to introduce cuts in the unemployment fund,
and in some salaries. Those of teachers were docked most
savagely, by 15 per cent. Right, teachers march to a
meeting to protest against this cut.

The National Government was formed by Ramsay
MacDonald after a majority in his Labour cabinet had
rejected a Budget proposal to cut the dole. This drastic
measure had been suggested in the face of a severe run on the
pound in 1931. Above, anxious crowds stand outside
Downing Street while the cabinet confer. The National
Government elected in 1931 not only failed to stop
unemployment (as promised in the election poster, right) but
introduced the Means Test—a bitterly resented system
whereby the thrifty were deprived of the dole.

Above, the Ace of Spades roadhouse on the Kingston by-pass.
Roadhouses on the outskirts of London, where you could eat,
drink and dance informally, were enormously popular
among the more raffish element, who could escape in their
motor cars from the restraints of traffic and convention.

Right, 'nippies' at Lyons Corner House reading
complimentary copies of the Daily Sketch. In the early
thirties, the newspaper giants started a cut-throat struggle
to boost their circulation—on which their advertising
revenue depended—with lures of free insurance and then
free gifts.

The thirties' craze for keeping fit. Right, a hikers' 'special'
leaving Paddington. The Youth Hostels Association was
founded in 1930 to cater for these swarms of hearty young
walkers, who tramped the countryside in a strange
assortment of clothes with rucksacks on their backs. In
London, too, people had more opportunity for enjoying fresh
air and exercise. Above, the Lido in Hyde Park opened by
George Lansbury, commissioner of works in the Second
Labour Government. Other amenities continued to be
provided for Londoners by the Labour-controlled LCC.

London night-life: above, a troupe of 'lovelies' at the Dorchester Hotel, who entertained diners to a cabaret turn. The Dorchester, built in 1930, soon became a favourite haunt of the 'top people' of the time. Less sophisticated amusement might be had from an evening at the theatre. Right, a scene from Eden's End *by J. B. Priestley, with Beatrix Lehmann and Ralph Richardson. Priestley was one of the most successful dramatists of the time, catering for an essentially middle-class, non-intellectual audience.*

The prelude to war: the Prime Minister, Neville Chamberlain, returns to London from Munich in September 1938. In his hand is the famous 'no-war' agreement with Hitler, guaranteeing the independence of Czechoslovakia.

Prelude to War

Royal events seem to dominate the middle of the 1930s in London. In 1935 the capital celebrated the Silver Jubilee of King George V. The king had wondered whether, because of the Depression, it was a good idea to celebrate this anniversary, but his modesty proved unnecessary. The grizzled old monarch drove not only to St Paul's, but through the poorest districts of the East End; they replied with banners—'Lousy but Loyal', ran one of them. Public buildings were floodlit, and houses and West End shops had their own flags and decorations.

The following year the king died, and he was brought that January to Westminster Hall for his lying-in-state. At one point his four sons, in their ceremonial military uniforms, stood vigil over their father's body. The new king, Edward VIII, had long been an ornament of London's night life, though he was equally diligent in touring the Empire and the distressed areas. Unlike his brothers, he had not married, and there was much romantic speculation over the bachelor monarch. His heart, however, was already captured, by an American divorcée, Mrs Simpson. On his accession, he was faced with an uncompromising choice between the throne and the marriage he desired; he chose the latter.

There were demonstrations in his favour in London: 'Stand by the King'. But abdication was inevitable, and he was succeeded by his brother as George VI, who brought with him to Buckingham Palace a wholesome family, including his daughter Elizabeth, now prospective heir to the throne. London was now able to stage the first Coronation of modern times, with sound film cameras and the microphones of the BBC carrying the ceremony to every corner of the globe. The street decorations and souvenirs, many designed for Edward VIII, were altered and up-dated, and things went splendidly. Clubland was aglow with illuminations, and the shopping centres again put on extravagant shows—Bond Street was hung with silken banners. Public buildings were floodlit again, as was the Home Fleet, which anchored in the Thames.

The focal point of the political system was secure once more. It was just as well, for a challenge to the traditional constitutional forms came from Sir Oswald Mosley, who organised the British Union of Fascists in 1934, a blackshirted para-military force run on German lines. There was a Chelsea headquarters, a bit like the Brown House in Munich. The government rushed through a Bill making political uniforms illegal, but the upraised arm of the Fascist salute and provocative processions through the Jewish quarters of the East End were now part of the London political scene. The Mosleyites also held monster rallies at Olympia and Earls Court, which in the early thirties had been most memorable for those rites of the new mass consumption markets, Radiolympia and the Motor Show.

Meanwhile, in more orderly fashion, the government of London had passed from Conservative supporters to the London Labour Party, which in 1934 captured the LCC. Under the leadership of Herbert Morrison the foundations were laid for a spell of uninterrupted control as long as that which the ousted party had enjoyed. All kinds of amenities were fostered, public assistance facilities were improved, and a subsidised housing scheme was introduced. A policy of the previous party, slum clearance, was also persevered with and medical services were improved. From 1935 the hospitals (many of which at that time were run by the LCC) were quietly extended and prepared, in co-operation with the government, for possible wartime use.

In the thirties the capital also acquired a unified public transport system. Herbert Morrison, as Minister of Transport in the second Labour Government, introduced a Bill in 1931 for the unification of all the transport undertakings in the London area, with the exception of the main-line railways. The LCC ceded its buses and trams, and the private companies their trams, buses and tubes. The Bill (taken over by the National Government, and eventually passed in 1933) created the London Passenger Transport Board, with a monopoly over its 2,000 square mile area. A single livery for buses and trams, the familiar red, and a single badge, the circle and bar, served the central area, and beyond into the Green Line belt.

A big programme of new works was almost immediately embarked upon; a little of Keynes's argument had filtered through to the government, who provided some of the money. Some of these extensions to the tube system were not in fact to be opened until the war had begun.

For now on the feeling that war might come was growing. In 1936 the sky of south London glowed. The Crystal Palace was on fire. It burned for hours, a gigantic free spectacle which people rushed to see in cars and buses. But this incineration of the great Victorian symbol of an Exhibition designed to celebrate international peace was a sinister omen of what was to come, particularly since rumour had it that the Palace had been deliberately destroyed because it was too conspicuous a land-mark.

The pacifists—led by Canon Sheppard, vicar of St Martin's-in-the-Fields—attempted to spread their creed by a Peace Ballot and a Peace Pledge Union and got over 100,000 to promise never to take up arms again. To counter this, Air Days were held at nearby aerodromes, like Hendon, and already some politicians like Churchill were reminding the nation of the dangerous times it was now living in. In the election of 1935 the National Government had been again returned, with a huge majority. The south of England in particular had supported them overwhelmingly. The government had in some ways deliberately played down the trigger-happy international situation, hoping that if Herr Hitler (who had a point) was appeased, all would be well.

The two themes jogged along in an uncomfortable counterpoint to each other. At one moment the 'sky looked dark'. Hitler walked out of the League of Nations, re-occupied the Rhineland and the Italians invaded Abyssinia. The next thing was that the papers and the radio were drooling over the 'Lambeth Walk', which took not only London but also America by storm. Sung by Lupino Lane in a show of 1937, *Me and My Girl*, at the Victoria Palace, it perpetuated the traditional view of cheerful Cockney behaviour, which Cockneys love to aid and abet themselves, with Pearly Kings and hop-picking in Kent. 'Knees Up Mother Brown' followed, keeping its popularity through the Blitz until it reached its apotheosis in East End street parties on VE Day.

'Will it be war?' was the question everyone asked in October 1938. Hitler was determined to take a large slice of Czechoslovakia. To allow him to do so would be to breach the Versailles settlement beyond repair. Britain and France were in effect guarantors of Czech territorial integrity. Neville Chamberlain, the Prime Minister, held that Britain was not ready for war, and that, anyway, it was not necessary to go to war over a strange country of which we knew nothing. But plans for Civil Defence and air raid precautions had been made. What was most feared was gas, which experts had predicted would be used against civilians in the cities as soon as war broke out. Cigarette card sets of the time instructed everyone how to detect mustard gas, and how to avoid contamination. The crisis grew. Barrage balloons flew over London from Regent's Park and other sites. Trenches were dug as protection against air-raids in Lincoln's Inn Fields, Hyde Park, Kensington Gardens and the suburban parks.

Londoners concluded they were for it, a front line target. The newsreels had shown them the German bombers strafing Spanish cities, and the Japanese bombing Shanghai. Thank goodness that the government had a scheme to get the children out, by evacuating them to country areas.

Then came the disgraceful anticlimax. The Prime Minister took off in an aircraft from London and flew to Munich. There he agreed to Hitler's demands. 'Peace in our time', he said on his return, and on leaving the aircraft waved the shameful piece of paper with his signature and Hitler's, by which the Czechs were betrayed, and Britain gained time.

A year later there was no piece of paper. On the hot morning of September 3, 1939, London and the world heard the same Prime Minister broadcast his declaration of war on Nazi Germany, now that she had invaded Poland. Immediately afterwards, the sirens sounded—a false alarm. But soon they were to sound in earnest, for London's nightly bombardment during the Blitz. The great city was to prove a frustrating target for the bombers of the Luftwaffe, a massive, curiously undaunted adversary, even when it seemed most defenceless. 'London Can Take It' was the slogan, and though much of the city was laid in ashes, the Germans were to spend a vital and irrecoverable part of their war effort in their air attack against it.

Above, the aging Bernard Shaw, the fiery Irish dramatist
and pioneer of Fabian socialism, is handed (in 1938) the
site deeds of a National Theatre in Kensington. No one
replaced Shaw as a literary and political pundit. Indeed,
until the thirties, when the effects of the depression and the
Spanish Civil War greatly multiplied the numbers of left-
wing intellectuals, writers took little interest in politics.
Prominent among the 'New Left' was the poet W. H. Auden.
Right, Auden setting out with Christopher Isherwood for the
Sino-Japanese war in 1938.

*Above, women demonstrate in favour of the king during the
Abdication crisis in December 1938. Many (including
Beaverbrook and Churchill) supported the king's decision to
marry Mrs Simpson, but the constitutional difficulties and
the disapproval of the 'Establishment' forced him to
abdicate. He married Mrs Simpson the following June.
Right, the Duke and Duchess of Windsor (as they became)
on their wedding day.*

Far right, Charlie Chaplin, perhaps the greatest star of the early cinema, in a scene from Modern Times (1936). The cinema transformed people's lives taking them from their homes and providing them with glamour and excitement. No other form of entertainment could compete. The theatre was hardest hit, although in the West End, Noel Coward was still assured of an audience. Right, Coward and Gertrude Lawrence in Tonight at 8.30.

Right, the ruins of the Crystal Palace, gutted by fire in December 1936—a presage of the fire-blackened debris of the Blitz. Another more solid portent of the coming struggle was the Admiralty Citadel, above, an air raid shelter for top people during the war.

Above, unemployed men singing in a London street in 1939. The unemployed still numbered more than a million in May 1940, and only disappeared as a problem in 1941. One of the cures was, of course, conscription, though this moved slowly in the first part of the war. Right, Hore Belisha, secretary of state for war, inspecting an early draft of soldiers in 1939.

Right, the king and queen visiting a badly bombed street in Fulham. The Blitz began in the autumn of 1940 and for eight weeks London was bombed every night. Morale, the Germans' main target, remained unbroken during the raids, although 30,000 civilians, more than half of them in London, were killed during the Blitz. ARP wardens were prominent among the efficiently organised anti-air-raid services. Above, ARP workers and others searching among piles of rubble after a raid in September 1940.

PICTURE SOURCES

Figures refer to page numbers
Associated Press, 126, 127; Batsford Ltd, 59; Central Press Photos, 97;
GLC, 65; Imperial War Museum, 35, 36; Radio Times Hulton Picture
Library, inside flap, 13, 14, 15, 16, 17, 18, 20, 21, 22-23, 24, 25, 26,
29, 30(T), 30(B), 31, 32, 33, 34, 38, 39, 40, 41, 60, 74, 77, 79 80(T),
80(B), 81, 82(B), 83, 84, 85, 86, 87, 88, 89, 90, 92, 98, 99, 100, 101,
102, 104, 106, 107, 108, 113, 115, 116, 117, 118, 119, 120, 121, 122,
123, 124, 125; Michael Taylor, 4, 44, 52, 53, 54, 55, 56, 57, 58, 61,
62, 63, 64, 66, 67; Topix, front cover, 37, 42, 43, 68, 75, 76, 82(T),
91, 103, 105, 114.   Map by Peter Sullivan

Picture research by Doris Bryen
Designed by Peter Williams

London Weekend Television Publications